3 8538 00014 9240

Stockton Twp Public Library
140 W. Benton Ave.
Stockton, IL. 61085-1312
     (815) 947-2030

DEMCO

Clay
v.
United States

Muhammad Ali
Objects to War

Suzanne Freedman

Landmark Supreme Court Cases

Enslow Publishers, Inc.

40 Industrial Road   PO Box 38
Box 398   Aldershot
Berkeley Heights, NJ 07922   Hants GU12 6BP
USA   UK

http://www.enslow.com

To my four wonderful grandchildren:
Sally, William, Hannah, and Erik

Copyright © 1997 by Suzanne Freedman

All rights reserved.

No part of this book may be reproduced by any means
without the written permission of the publisher.

Library of Congress Cataloging-in-Publication Data

Freedman, Suzanne, 1932–
    Clay v. United States: Muhammad Ali objects to war / Suzanne
Freedman.
        p. cm. — (Landmark Supreme Court cases)
    Includes bibliographical references and index.
    Summary: Describes the trial of Muhammad Ali, the first three-time boxing
Heavyweight Champion of the World, for refusing to serve in the Vietnam War.
    ISBN 0-89490-855-3
        1. Ali, Muhammad, 1942–   —Trials, litigation, etc.—Juvenile
literature. 2. Trials (Political crimes and offenses)—United States—
Juvenile literature. 3. Conscientious objectors—Legal status, laws,
etc.—United States—Juvenile literature. [1. Ali, Muhammad, 1942–
—Trials litigation, etc. 2. Trials (Political crimes and offenses) 3.Conscientious
Objectors. 4. Afro-Americans—Biography.] I. Title. II. Title: Clay versus
United States. III. Series.
KF224.A47F74   1997
343.73'0126'0269—dc21   97-9985
                                                            CIP
                                                             AC
Printed in the United States of America

10 9 8 7 6 5 4 3

Photo Credits: Harris & Ewing/Collection of the Supreme Court of the United
States, p. 71; Reproduced from the collections of the Library of Congress, pp. 20,
32, 48, 66, 91, 97; Robert Haggins, Schomburg Center for Research in Black
Culture, p. 12; Ted Gray, Schomburg Center for Research in Black Culture, New
York Public Library, pp. 9, 82, 85; UPI/BETTMANN, pp. 21, 36, 55, 58, 74.

Cover Photo: Ted Gray/Schomburg Center for Research in Black Culture, New
York Public Library (inset). Franz Jantzen "Collection of the Supreme Court of the
United States" (background).

Contents

6-4-14

Acknowledgments

To the following people, for their invaluable assistance and encouragement:

Maya Keech, Photographs and Print Division, Library of Congress; Sue Ford, Librarian, New Milford Library, New Milford, CT; Thomas Valluzzo, D.M.D.; John Alexander Strickland.

1

Private Ali or Private Citizen?

On February 5, 1964, boxer Cassius Marcellus Clay, just nineteen days past his twenty-second birthday, defeated Sonny Liston in Miami Beach, Florida. He knocked him out in fifteen rounds to become the new World Heavyweight Champion. It was a day different from any other day in his life. Black Muslim Minister Malcolm X had come to see him fight. Malcolm X, born Malcolm Little in Omaha, Nebraska, in 1925, joined the Black Muslims when he was twenty-seven. He became a recruiter and activist, changed his name, and by 1959 had attracted national attention with his writings about the Islam faith. Clay's manager burst into his dressing room shouting, "Do you know who's out there? . . . we've got to get him out of here! [If] the newspapers know you're associated with Muslims like Malcolm X, your career is over. . . ."[1]

What his manager did not know was that Malcolm X was not the only X in the room. Clay had been quietly studying the precepts of the Islam religion and meeting with representatives of an African-American religious group known as the Lost-Found Nation of Islam. In the summer of 1963, Cassius Clay secretly changed his name—first to Cassius X, then to Muhammad Ali. To the public he was still known as Cassius Clay, but to other Black Muslims, he was Muhammad Ali.

Muslim preachers insisted that members drop their surnames, which they said were not the original names of their ancestors from Africa but the names of slave owners. They could adopt instead, the letter X, which would stand for their lost African name, or they could take an appropriate Muslim name.

There was a press conference after the fight. Ali was asked about the Selective Service exams he had taken on January 24, 1964, to determine whether he was eligible for military service. He told reporters he had not yet received the results. The press then wanted to ask Ali some questions about the fight. "Were you surprised you won?" someone asked. Ali replied no; he was the better boxer. Then someone asked, "Are you a card-carrying member of the Black Muslims?"[2] Ali replied, "I believe in Allah and in peace. . . . Followers of Allah . . . don't carry knives. They don't tote weapons . . . you can't condemn a man for wanting peace. If you do, you condemn peace itself. . . ."[3] Malcolm X became Muhammad Ali's constant companion after the championship fight and after the announcement of Ali's allegiance to the Nation of Islam as it was practiced by the Black Muslims.

The Nation of Islam was founded in the early 1930s by Wallace Fard in Detroit, Michigan. Four years later, Fard mysteriously disappeared. Elijah Muhammad became the head of the Nation of Islam in Chicago, Illinois. The first time Ali heard about Elijah Muhammad was in 1959, in Chicago. He read *Muhammad Speaks*, the Nation of Islam's newspaper, and something clicked. Two years later when he was in training for a fight in Miami, Ali met a man named Captain Sam at Red's Barbershop in the Overtown section of Miami, where Sam worked as the main recruiter for a new religion—Islam. Ali's brother Rudy had already signed on. If Sam signed Ali up, it would be a big boost for the Black Muslims, so Sam began a campaign to recruit Ali.

Sam invited Ali to a meeting at a Muslim mosque.

(A mosque is a building used for public worship by Muslims.) Ali began to seriously consider becoming a Muslim. Islam, the name given to the religion practiced by Muslims, requires submission to the will of Allah (God) whose primary mission is spreading the word of peace. The idea of peace dominates the Islamic faith. It is a religion of peace. The Muslim emblem, the crescent, stands for freedom, justice, and equality.

Prayers are recited at sunrise, noon, mid-afternoon, sundown, and before retiring. If one awakens during the night, another prayer is made. In fact, two prayers should be said during the night, making a total of seven a day. There is no Sabbath or day of rest in Islam. All days are worship days. Muslims are also expected to wash and clean all exposed body parts before early morning prayer.

Many African Americans believed that the Nation of Islam, led by Elijah Muhammad, would enlighten them. When Elijah Muhammad died in 1975, Elijah Muhammad's son, W. Deen Muhammad, took over the leadership of the Nation of Islam. He called for a "new sense of patriotism" urging African Americans to "identify with the land and flag."[4] His goal was to bring Islam into the mainstream of American life.[5]

In the early 1960s the Nation of Islam, under Elijah Muhammad, taught separation of black and

Muhammad Ali is shown here eulogizing the honorable Elijah Muhammad on Savior's Day at Jones Armory in Chicago, Illinois. After the death of Elijah Muhammad, the Black Muslims formed several separate religious organizations.

white Americans. The group, whose members are called Black Muslims, viewed whites as blue-eyed devils who were responsible for the problems of African Americans all over the world. The Black Muslims at one time wanted a separate state for blacks within the United States.[6]

A radically different phase began under W. Deen Muhammad. He abandoned unorthodox notions that had presented obstacles for other Muslims' recognition of this movement as being authentically Islamic. In May 1985, the American Muslim Mission was dissolved to unify its members with the worldwide Muslim community.[7]

W. Deen Muhammad rejected some of his father's teachings. Since then the movement has splintered into different groups. The ministry of Louis Farrakhan remains closer to Elijah Muhammad's beliefs. Farrakhan is the current leader of the Nation of Islam. The controversial Farrakhan has offended many blacks and whites with anti-Semitic and racial slurs. Yet the Nation's successful work with young people in inner-city African-American communities has been admired even by some critics. Muhammad has urged Farrakhan's followers to put aside their idea of a separate nation and to join the Muslim mainstream in which everyone can accept each other as equals.

"The first time I felt truly spiritual . . . was when I walked into the Muslim Temple [mosque] in Miami,"[8] Ali remembered. He began reading *Muhammad Speaks*, the Nation of Islam's newspaper, every week. He continued to attend meetings. Eventually, he was introduced to his teacher, Jeremiah Shabazz. Shabazz was the Nation of Islam's "minister over the Deep South" (the states of Georgia, South Carolina, Alabama, Mississippi, Louisiana, and Florida).

In the movement's early years, the Nation of Islam believed that the white man personified evil. It was the white man who had enslaved blacks. The white man was the devil and a doomed race. Muhammad Ali became a follower of this doctrine.[9]

Elijah Muhammad liked Muhammad Ali. Elijah Muhammad knew Ali to be a man who could validate the religion, make it credible, and recruit large numbers into its ranks. He announced in a radio broadcast from Chicago on March 6, 1964: "The Clay name has no divine meaning. . . .'Muhammad Ali' is what I will give him for as long as he believes in Allah and follows me."[10] Ali responded, "I was honored that Elijah Muhammad gave me a truly beautiful name. 'Muhammad' means one worthy of praise; 'Ali' was the name of a great general."[11]

For three years before the Liston fight in 1964, Ali

Heavyweight champ Muhammad Ali proclaims to the world that he is Muslim, and a follower of Elijah Muhammad.

was sneaking into Nation of Islam meetings through the back door. He did not want anyone to know he was there. He was afraid that if people found out, he would not be allowed to fight for the heavyweight title.[12]

The same year, 1961, Ali and his brother Rudy drove from Miami, Florida, to Detroit, Michigan, to hear Elijah Muhammad speak. Ali met Muslim Minister Malcolm X for the first time at a Muslim mosque there. The two became friends. Malcolm X always left his audiences spellbound. He appealed to a growing number of African-American writers, artists, and intellectuals. He was known all over the country and appeared many times on televised debates to speak out against discrimination toward African Americans.

Malcolm X felt that Ali's conversion would not conflict with his boxing career. His religion should be his own concern, even though the Nation of Islam was against all forms of sports. A Muslim rally was about the world's last place to find fight fans.

In late 1963 the Nation of Islam was being torn apart. There was a bitter difference of opinion between Malcolm X and Elijah Muhammad; Malcolm X began to question the road the Nation of Islam was taking. Members of the Nation began to take sides. Ali sided with Elijah Muhammad, who, he believed, was Allah's messenger. Malcolm X established his own group called the Organization of African-American Unity. He was later assassinated on February 21, 1965.

Muhammad Ali's father believed that the faith had too much control over his son's life. Both of Ali's parents thought he had joined a strange cult they did not know about or like. Ali's father argued that the Muslims were only after his son's money, but Ali could never say anything bad about Elijah Muhammad. His religion brought him an inner peace. "All they [Muslims] want to do is live in peace with the world. They don't want to stir up any kind of trouble. . . ."[13]

On April 18, 1960, eighteen-year-old Muhammad Ali registered, as required at that time, for military service with his local Selective Service board in his hometown of Louisville, Kentucky. On March 9, 1962, he was classified 1-A (available for draft). On January 24, 1964, he was ordered to report to the Armed Forces Induction Center in Coral Gables, Florida. Here he would take an aptitude test to determine if he met the qualifications for military service.

Ali had been a poor reader and speller in high school. He had trouble with the exam, especially the math section. The result showed nineteen correct answers out of a total of seventy-eight questions. This was well below the passing grade of thirty correct answers. He was retested, and he failed once more. On March 26, 1964, he was reclassified 1-Y (not qualified under current standards for service in the armed forces). Secretary of the Army, Stephen Ailes, wrote to the chairman of the House of Representatives Armed Service Committee, Carl Vinson, ". . . [I]t was my decision that Cassius Clay should be rejected for induction due to his inability to meet prescribed minimum standards."[14]

In the early part of 1966, the war in Vietnam was getting more intense. The Army mental aptitude passing grade was lowered from 30 to 15, which meant that Ali would now be eligible for the draft. On February 14, Ali's lawyer appeared before the local board in Louisville, requesting a postponement of or deferment from military service. Three days later, the request was denied. Ali was reclassified 1-A. He was twenty-four years old.

On March 17, 1966, Ali appeared before the local draft board to request conscientious objector status. A conscientious objector is someone who claims that personal beliefs prevent him or her from bearing arms in this country's armed forces. As a Black Muslim, Ali did not believe in war in any form. His request for conscientious objector status was denied, and six weeks later, the denial was upheld on appeal.

On August 23, 1966, Ali appeared at a special hearing. The hearing officer was Judge Lawrence Grauman. He had served on a Kentucky Circuit Court for some twenty-five years. He was to hear evidence and consider the merits of Ali's application. He would then issue recommendations to the Kentucky Appeal Board. In order to be eligible for conscientious objector status, Ali had to convince Grauman that his objection to military service was sincere, that it was based on religious training and belief, and that he was opposed to participation in all wars of any kind.

Ali handed Grauman a twenty-one page letter outlining his religious beliefs. Then he testified under oath: "the teachings of the Honorable Elijah Muhammad tell us . . . that we are not to participate in wars on the side of nonbelievers, and this [Vietnam] is a Christian country . . . not a Muslim country. . . ."[15]

Grauman ruled that Ali was "of good character, morals and integrity and sincere in his objection on religious grounds to participation in war in any form."[16] He recommended that Ali's conscientious objector status be granted.

The Department of Justice, however, advised the Kentucky Appeal Board that the claim should be denied "for failure to satisfy each of the three basic tests for qualification as a conscientious objector."[17] The Board denied Ali's claim without giving any reasons.

On August 25, 1966, L. Mendel Rivers, Chairman of the House Armed Services Committee, addressed a Veterans of Foreign Wars audience:

> Listen to this. If that great theologian of Black Muslim power . . . is deferred, you watch what happens in Washington . . . what has happened to the leadership of our nation when a man, any man regardless of color, can . . . advise his listeners to tell the President when he is called to serve in the armed forces, . . . 'I'm not going.'[18]

"How can I kill somebody when I pray five times a day for peace?" Ali asked.[19] Two weeks after Ali's successful fight with Ernie Terrell, Congressman Robert Michel of Illinois condemned Ali on the floor of the House of Representatives:

> I cannot understand how patriotic Americans can promote, or pay for, pugilistic [boxing] exhibitions by an individual who has become the symbol of draft evasion. While thousands of our finest young men are fighting and dying in the jungles of Vietnam, this healthy specimen is profiteering from a series of shabby bouts. Apparently he [Ali] will fight anyone but the Vietcong.[20]

Ali continued to argue for his status as a conscientious objector. On March 6, 1967, the National

Selective Service Presidential Appeal Board unanimously voted to maintain his 1-A classification, making him eligible for military service. Eight days later, on April 11, Ali was ordered to report for induction in Louisville. Ali's lawyers had the date and place changed to April 28, in Houston, Texas. Houston was thought to be more friendly to Ali.

It suddenly became clear that Ali might have to leave the boxing world to enlist in the service. He consulted with his manager and Muslim spiritual advisor, Herbert Muhammad, who was one of six sons of Elijah Muhammad. "I have nothing to lose by standing up and following my own beliefs. I'll go down in history." Ali said:

> I'm a 1000% religious man. If I thought goin' to war would bring freedom, justice and equality to 22 million Negroes, they wouldn't have to draft me.[21]

Ali seemed resigned to the idea of going to jail for standing up for his beliefs. He had to make the decision on his own, but he also hoped to remain in Elijah Muhammad's good graces. (Elijah Muhammad had served three years in a federal prison because he had refused to register for the draft during World War II.)[22]

Meanwhile, African-American voices across the nation had grown more bitter and began to speak out about the draft and the war in Vietnam. As the war continued to consume the country, African-American civil rights leader Dr. Martin Luther King, Jr., broadened his criticisms of American society. He saw the Vietnam War's impact on the resources of the United States.

Meanwhile answers to the question of what would happen to Ali if he refused to be drafted remained unclear. Bail could be set, an actual date announced, and Ali might be convicted. Ali, however, had faith in the Nation of Islam and the will of Allah.

Muhammad Ali's lawyers were Quinnon Hodges from Houston, Hayden Covington from New York, and Chauncey Eskridge from Chicago. They arrived with Ali at the United States Customs House in Houston, Texas, at 8:30 A.M. on April 28, 1967. The steps of the buildings were filled with people. Students from Texas Southern University were marching with banners that read "STAY HOME, MUHAMMAD ALI."[23] An elderly lady cut through the crowd to whisper, "Stand up, Brother. We're with you! Fight for us! Don't let us down." A band of long-haired hippies shouted, "We didn't go! You don't go!"[24]

A group of police pushed the crowd back from the doors. Muhammad Ali climbed the steps. A Navy officer escorted him into a room about half the size of

Muhammad Ali is shown here next to attorney Hayden Covington, as they file a petition with the clerk.

a basketball court. Ali stood silently with the other thirty recruits in a line. A group of officers in front of him was sorting through papers and checking lists. Ali had to take a written test, undergo a physical examination, and then wait to be called for induction. Lieutenant Steven Dunkley, a young officer, stood behind an oak wood podium surrounded on both sides by American flags. Dunkley began to read a prepared statement:

> You are about to be inducted into the Armed Forces of the United States, in the Army, the Navy, the Air Force or the Marine Corps, as indicated by the service

Heavyweight champion Muhammad Ali arrives at the Army Induction Center where he is scheduled to be inducted into the Army. Ali has said he will refuse induction thereby leaving himself open to criminal prosecution.

announced following your name when called. You will take one step forward as your name and service are called and such step will constitute your induction into the armed forces indicated.[25]

For months, Ali had tried to prepare himself for this moment. He felt nervous. He hoped no one would notice that his shoulders trembled.[26] He remembered the words of Herbert Muhammad:

> Whatever that choice is, you've got to accept the outcome of your own decision . . . this decision you make will determine the future of your life . . . all I can say is, may Allah be with you, and when Allah is with you, no one can defeat you . . . If you feel what you have decided to do is right, then be a man and stand up for it . . . Declare the truth and die for it.[27]

"Cassius Clay—Army!"

2

War and Conscientious Objectors

In 1658 Richard Keene, a Quaker from Maryland, refused to participate in training for the colonial militia. Keene objected to military activities because of his religious beliefs. By standing up for his antiwar principles, Keene became the first-known "conscientious objector" in the British colonies.

Historically, the conscientious objector in the United States has been a member of a religious sect whose principles forbid the use of weapons in war, or any active support of war. In colonial America the Quakers in Rhode Island, North Carolina, New Jersey, and Pennsylvania were all pacifists, people opposed to war. The Mennonites came to America in 1683 followed by smaller sects around 1719.

Mennonites are part of the historic peace church tradition. From the beginning, followers were committed to the principle of nonresistance. After reading the Bible and examining the record of the early church, the first Mennonites came to believe that they could not participate in war of any kind.

Throughout their history, Mennonites have sought assurance from the government that they would not have to participate in warfare. Mennonites first received exemption from military service in Canada, in 1793. The first parliament of Upper Canada was eager to attract Mennonite settlers from the United States. In an effort to do this, it exempted them from yearly military exercises. However, the parliament imposed a tax that conscientious objectors would have to pay instead of participating in the military. Mennonites, together with the Quakers, not only opposed participating in the military, they opposed paying for it, too.

These exemptions allowed Mennonites in Canada and elsewhere to avoid military service during World War I (1914–1918). When World War II began in 1939 the idea of alternative service was created. This enabled some eleven thousand conscientious objectors (COs), including seventy-five hundred Mennonites and Quakers, to perform public works such as essential forestry, farming, and industrial work instead of entering the service. Mennonite women also contributed to peace by preparing aid packages for people suffering from the effects of war.

As early as 1754, the Quakers, who called themselves the Society of Friends, strengthened their commitment to peace. They were abolitionists, they began to denounce slavery. Since the Revolutionary War of 1776, many Quakers had placed patriotism first. At the time of the Civil War (1861–1865), many regarded the abolition of slavery as more important than the evils of war. During World War I, those who were not willing to bear arms performed relief work or medical service. During World War II, the question of military service was left to the individual's conscience. Efforts toward eliminating the basic causes of war became the Quakers' most significant work.

Mennonites today are concerned with finding ways to make peace, not just finding ways to avoid war. These ways include relief and development work around the world, service in inner cities, operation of mediation agencies, and victim/offender reconciliation programs.

At least some recognition of the right of these religious sects to abstain from military service was granted by Massachusetts (1661), Rhode Island (1673), and Pennsylvania (1757). These states allowed those with "conscientious scruples" to refrain from bearing arms.

During the French and Indian Wars (1689–1763), the state of Virginia imprisoned a small group of Quakers for failing to cooperate with a 1756 Virginia Militia Law. The law required all young men to participate in a lottery and to draw draft lots. Seven Quakers refused. They were jailed. After spending a week in jail, they were brought before a court where they "asserted [their] readiness to comply with the law in all things not against [their] conscience but to bear arms or fight we could not."[1] The objectors were taken to Colonel George Washington's headquarters. There, Virginia Governor Robert Dinwiddle tried to convince Washington to put the group in a stockade until they became reasonable. Washington, however, was moved by the courage and determination of the objectors. He ordered all seven people freed and granted them permission to live with local Quakers until their militia obligation ended.

In nearly every war in United States history, there have been soldiers who were unwilling to serve for different reasons. During the American Revolutionary War (1775–1783), when the thirteen colonies on the Atlantic seaboard of North America won independence from Great Britain and became the United States,

Quakers, Mennonites, and other members of "peace churches" tried to avoid the colonial draft.

The first nationwide draft by the federal government came in 1863 in the middle of the American Civil War. This war was waged between the Confederacy—southern states trying to preserve slavery and an agricultural way of life and the Union—northern states dedicated to a more modern way of life, and to ending slavery.

President Abraham Lincoln was sympathetic to conscientious objectors. He pushed a bill through Congress that acknowledged the validity of conscientious objectors' desires. The bill stated that they could perform alternative service in hospitals. Many pacifists, however, refused to perform such service. They still considered it an active support of the war.

The Federal Militia Act of 1862 allowed draft exemptions for those considered physically, mentally, or morally incapable of serving. There were also two other alternatives provided for those who had the money to use them: draftees could avoid service by paying three hundred dollars or by hiring a substitute for a mutually agreed upon fee.

While the draft during the Civil War did not actually produce many troops, it did result in bloody riots in many major northern cities. Some rioters protested the draft. Others protested the war itself. The Confederacy instituted a draft in 1863 with fewer loopholes than the Union draft. But it, too, was not very effective. When the United States went to war with Spain in 1898 the draft was forsaken entirely in favor of locally raised volunteer forces.

Less than twenty years later, when World War I began in 1914, the draft was brought back. Nearly 72 percent of the 3.5 million soldiers who served in World War I were draftees. The government depended more on the draft during World War I than during previous wars. It also treated those who objected to the draft more harshly than in the past. In April 1918, the War Department ordered all conscientious objectors to be court-martialed. Four hundred fifty conscientious objectors were found guilty. Of these, seventeen received death sentences (but were later pardoned), one hundred forty-two were sentenced to life in prison. Seventy-three received twenty year terms and only fifteen received jail terms of three years or less.[2]

World War I brought a Selective Service Act that provided exemption for the religious conscientious objectors, but it demanded noncombatant service of any kind specified by the President and the secretary of war. Many conscientious objectors would not cooperate in any way with the war effort; hundreds were sent to prison.

The World War I draft was different from past drafts: the rich could no longer hire substitutes. Those in more important jobs, however, that is those who generally made the most money, were frequently exempted from service. The draft was much less an issue in World War II (1939–1945). Of the 3.5 million men who registered, only about seventy-two thousand, less than two-tenths of one percent, requested conscientious objector status. Though being a conscientious objector in the first half of the 1940s was not socially popular, objectors received much better treatment than in World War I. Just over six thousand conscientious objectors were sent to prison.

By 1917, a new type of conscientious objector appeared. He was often an agnostic or atheist. (An agnostic is one who does not know whether or not God exists. An atheist is someone who denies that God exists.) He based his refusal to serve on political, social, or personal beliefs. The philosophical basis for this position had been part of American thought for almost seventy-five years. It was outlined by American writer Henry David Thoreau in his essay *Civil Disobedience*. Thoreau went to jail in 1846 as a protest against the Mexican War and the extension of slavery. He refused to pay his taxes to support an unjust war. He was confined in a Concord, Massachusetts, jail. Thoreau wrote, "The true man of conscience, whether motivated by religious or secular scruples, not only had the obligation to refrain from acts that violated his conscience but the obligation actively to disobey laws that told him to violate that conscience."[3]

Mandatory enrollment into the armed forces, in the form of the Draft Act, was instituted by the United States Congress in 1917. Those men who objected to war for religious reasons would be exempt from military service. The exemptions, however, included only those who belonged to a "well recognized religious sect or organization . . . whose existing creed or principles [forbade] its members to participate in war in any form."[4] (More than one hundred thousand applications were filed with local draft boards for conscientious objector status in 1970. Of that number, nineteen thousand were granted conscientious objector status. There were more conscientious objector applications in 1970 than during World War I and World War II combined.[5])

On March 17, 1948, as the Cold War between the United States and the former Soviet Union emerged from the ruins of World War II, President Harry S. Truman called both houses of Congress together and asked for a resumption of the draft. Although the

United States did not go to war with the former Soviet Union, war did break out five years later in Korea. Once again, the great majority of those who served in the armed forces were draftees.

America's next war, in Vietnam, would prove to be the undoing of the draft. As opposition to the war grew in the late 1960s and early 1970s, the draft became a major focus of protesters. Many Americans felt that their country's conduct in Vietnam was unjust and brutal. Thousands of draft dodgers and deserters fled to Canada, Europe, and Sweden. Between 1964 and 1965 draft-card burning became fashionable. Congress reacted sharply to this new type of protest. In 1965, they passed a law that made the destruction of draft cards illegal. (Forty-six people were prosecuted under the law; thirty-three were convicted.)[6]

The elimination of student deferments—a program under which many of the children of the middle and upper class parents had avoided service in order to continue their education—in addition to the introduction of a draft lottery in 1970 added to the opposition to the draft. As the war became more unpopular the courts seemed to adopt a new attitude toward draft resisters. The Pentagon issued a draft call on September 29 for ten thousand men during the last three months of

A follower of Muhammad Ali shows support for the champ outside the induction center in Houston, Texas.

1971. It was the first call-up since President Nixon signed the draft bill extending the draft for two years.

Douglas Clyde Macintosh was a Canadian by birth. He first came to the United States as a graduate student. In 1907 he was ordained as a Baptist minister. In 1909 he began to teach at Yale University in New Haven, Connecticut. He was the chaplain of the Yale Graduate School. He was also a professor of theology (religion), and he served as a chaplain with the Canadian Army after the start of World War I.

In 1925, Macintosh declared his intention to become an American citizen. The Connecticut Federal Court denied his application on the grounds that he would not promise in advance to bear arms in defense of the United States unless he believed the war to be morally justified.

Five Supreme Court Justices held that the naturalization law could be interpreted to require Macintosh to declare his unqualified willingness to bear arms. (Naturalization is the process by which people born in another country become citizens.) In a dissenting opinion, Chief Justice Charles Evans Hughes argued that the law did not require an oath that the applicant bear arms. Respect for religious conviction and our national history of tolerance for conscientious objection counseled the Court to interpret the law favorably to the applicant.[7]

The war in Vietnam produced a new kind of conscientious objector, one who does not condemn all violence or even all wars, just one specific war. Even before January 1, 1961—the date from which official counts of Americans lost in the Vietnam War are kept—the United States had taken an active role, if still a largely backseat one, in Southeast Asia. In 1954, Vietnam had ended a long period of French colonialism, but at the price of a divided country, it won the promise of free elections and unification. It became clear that Ho Chi Minh, the Vietnamese political leader who would preside over the war with South Vietnam and the United States from 1959 to 1969, would win such an election. The United States went on record as opposing the election of Ho Chi Minh who was an avowed Communist. Within months war broke out between North and South Vietnam. Throughout the administrations of Presidents Dwight D. Eisenhower and John F. Kennedy, the United States sided more and more with the Republic of South Vietnam, sending military advisors there. After the Gulf of Tonkin incident, in August 1964 (two United States destroyers had been attacked by North Vietnamese torpedo boats), United States military forces were sent to Vietnam.

Between 1964 and 1973, the war in Vietnam divided the United States as no issue had since the Civil War. People were divided by age, by social status, by race, and by political opinion. On one side were those who insisted that if South Vietnam were allowed to fall to a Communist power, the rest of Southeast Asia would eventually follow. The other side maintained that the struggle within Vietnam was basically an internal civil war and that the United States should stay out of it. Either way, tens of thousands of Vietnamese, Americans, and others—soldiers and civilians—died or had their lives shattered by their experiences during the Vietnam War.

By 1964, many young Americans from various racial backgrounds strongly disagreed with our country's policy in Southeast Asia. Ali's conversion to the Nation of Islam upset many of his followers. Many were angry about his stand on Vietnam. He received threatening phone calls, hostile letters, and telegrams: "You have disgraced your title," one telegram said, "and the American flag. . . ."[8] A former heavyweight champ wrote "Apologize for your unpatriotic remark[s] or you'll be barred from the ring.[9] Many, like Muhammad Ali, were willing to express their disagreements no matter what the consequences. They did this by refusing to be drafted. They were willing to risk a five-year prison sentence or the possibility of a long exile. Some chose to avoid the draft by leaving the country.

A cease-fire on January 27, 1973, marked the first drawn-out stage of the end of the war. The Vietnam War officially came to an end on April 30, 1975. Even after that, however, its effects remained in the forefront of American life. Vietnam veterans struggled to rebuild the lives that had been painfully interrupted.

Actually, the antiwar movement represented one of many great changes that were sweeping the country in

Muhammad Ali is shown here with his teacher, Elijah Muhammad. When Ali joined the Nation of Islam he upset many of his fans.

the 1960s. The civil rights movement, which attacked racism through large-scale demonstrations, changed relations between black and white Americans forever.

America's youth became more critical of the flaws in our society and culture. Old established moral codes and rules were being challenged everywhere. It was the Vietnam War, however, more than anything else, that symbolized to a generation of rebellious Americans what had gone wrong with their country. By 1967, Americans saw the Vietnam War as a major skirmish at the edge of a civilized world. The United States Government was spending $2 billion a month on the war and had some four hunded fifty thousand men troops stationed in Vietnam.[10]

Every week almost one hundred American soldiers died fighting in Vietnam. More than five hundred soldiers were wounded each week.[11] This drama of human suffering was televised every night in the homes of millions of Americans.

If he had agreed to be drafted, Ali would have spent thirty days overseas entertaining the troops and then would have returned home to the boxing ring. Perhaps, if Ali had not become a Muslim, he might have consented to such a deal.[12]

The peace movement expanded as the Vietnam War raged on. Teach-ins and marches were followed by sit-ins and lie-ins, draft card burnings, and demonstrations. There were desertions from the Army and other acts of civil disobedience. The country was in turmoil. Vietnam was not a world war, but a battle in a small country against an enemy whose military power could in no way be compared to that of the United States. Nonetheless, the war continued with no sign that communist forces would give up. President Lyndon Johnson took a moderate course in Vietnam so he could be assured a place in history.

His moderate course was attacked by both those against the war and those who agreed that our national security was at stake and that victory could be achieved only by use of massive military power against North Vietnam.

By the end of 1967 Americans had grown uneasy about Johnson's policy: some advocated withdrawal, others escalation. They grew impatient about the stalemate in Vietnam. A majority of Americans polled thought it had been a mistake getting involved in Vietnam and approval of the President's handling of the war slipped to 28 percent.[13] The American people were having second thoughts about the President.

The promise of an easy victory was no longer guaranteed. Public support waned. The press turned against Johnson. Some members of Johnson's cabinet, Secretary of Health, Education, and Welfare John Gardiner and Secretary of Labor Willard Wirtz, expressed doubts to the President about United States policy, but Johnson did not want to hear other people's doubts.

The peace movement was largely made up of the younger generation, some of whom interpreted the Vietnam situation as a civil war within a single tiny country. They saw what happened there as having little relation to what happened in the rest of Southeast Asia. Johnson lost the ability to communicate with the members of the peace movement.

Unhappiness about the war and the protesters attached itself to the President. The country was in a state of unrest and Johnson was blamed for it. The turbulent 1960s became Johnson's problem and he began to consider removing himself from public office. On March 31, 1968, he stunned a nationwide television audience with a broadcast from the White House ". . . I shall not seek, and will not accept, the nomination of my [Democratic] party for another term as your President."[14]

The following day, Johnson was savoring flash reports. A popular poll revealed a complete reversal in his popularity rating; from 57 percent disapproval before the March 31 speech to 57 percent approval after it.[15]

In Vietnam, there was no change; a stalemate

continued on the battlefield and at the peace table. Johnson's political rival Robert Kennedy was killed in June 1968. His chosen successor, Hubert Humphrey, was not doing well in the polls. Richard Nixon ran successfully against Humphrey, winning in a very close race. He took office on January 20, 1969, to become the thirty-seventh President of the United States.

On August 31, 1971, Deputy Secretary of Defense David M. Packard signed a directive broadening the Pentagon's guidelines on conscientious objectors. It would now include "deeply held moral or ethical beliefs" as grounds for discharge as set down in the 1970 Supreme Court decision *Welsh* v. *United States.*

Under the new guidelines, servicemen applying for discharge as conscientious objectors on the basis of their "religious training and belief" need not express belief in a Supreme Being. The Supreme Court in *Welsh* v. *United States*, had ruled that a young man who specifically disavowed a religious basis for his antiwar beliefs was entitled to conscientious objector status if he sincerely objected to all wars. The Court held that the draft law did not limit conscientious objector status to those belonging to a religious group that opposed war. In the case of Elliot A. Welsh, II the draft law exempted "registrants whose consciences, spurred by deeply held moral, ethical or religious beliefs, would give them no rest or peace if they allowed themselves to become a part of [an] instrument of war."[16]

In the prevailing opinion, Justice Hugo L. Black said that in both *United States* v. *Seeger* (1965) and the *Welsh* case (1970) the selective service system denied conscientious objector status because of an absence of religious basis for the registrants anti-war beliefs. He said conscientious objector status should not be denied to someone "whose conscientious objection to participation in all wars is founded to a substantial extent upon consideration of public policy."[17]

The Supreme Court stated in *United States* v. *Seeger*, in 1965, that:

> The test of belief in a relation to a Supreme Being is whether a given belief that is sincere and meaningful occupies a place . . . parallel to that filled by the orthodox belief in God of one who clearly qualifies for exemption.[18]

In the 1970 majority opinion of the Supreme Court, in *Welsh* v. *United States*, Justice Hugo Black wrote:

> What is necessary for . . . conscientious objection to all war is that this opposition to war stem from . . . [his] moral, ethical or religious beliefs about what is right or wrong and that these beliefs be held with the strength of traditional religious convictions . . .[19]

The *Seeger* decision in 1965 and the *Welsh* decision in 1970 declared that those with moral and ethical objections to war in any form have the same right as religious objectors to refuse to enter into combat. The current Military Service Act of 1971 (formerly the Universal Military Training and Service Act) was revised by Congress after the Supreme Court decisions on *Seeger* and *Welsh*. It read in part:

> Nothing . . . shall be construed to require any person to be subject to combatant training and service in the Armed Forces of the United States who, by reason of religious training and belief, is conscientiously opposed to participation in war in any form . . .[20] [i.e., belief in an individual's relation to a supreme being involving duties beyond a human relationship but not essentially political, sociological or philosophical views or a merely personal moral code.]

Daniel Andrew Seeger was convicted in a New York federal court for having refused induction in the armed forces. He was originally classified 1-A in 1953, and his classification was changed two years later to 2-S (student). He remained at this status until 1958, when he was reclassified 1-A. Seeger first claimed exemption as a conscientious objector in 1957, when he declared he was "conscientiously opposed to participation in war in any form by reason of his 'religious' belief. . . ."[21]

Seeger cited famous philosophers Plato, Aristotle, and Spinoza in support of his ethical belief in intellectual and moral integrity. His belief was found to be sincere, honest, and made in good faith, but Seeger's claim was denied. It was not based upon a "belief in a relation to a supreme being" as required by Section 6(j) of the Military Service Act. At the trial, Seeger admitted that his belief was not in relation to a Supreme Being as commonly understood. He was convicted.

The controlling facts in *Welsh* v. *United States* are strikingly similar to those in *United States* v. *Seeger*. Both Seeger and Welsh were raised in religious homes. Both attended church in their childhood. Neither church, however, taught its members not to engage in war at any time for any reason. Neither Seeger nor Welsh continued his childhood religious ties into young adulthood. Neither belonged to any religious groups or adhered to the teachings of any organized religion during the period of his involvement with the Selective Service System. At the time of draft registration, neither had yet come to accept pacifist principles. Both men's views on war developed only in subsequent years. When their ideas did fully mature, however, both applied to their local draft boards for conscientious objector exemptions from military service under Section 6(j) of the Universal Military Training and Service Act.

Neither Seeger nor Walsh could definitely affirm or deny that he believed in a "supreme being." Both, however, affirmed that they held deep conscientious scruples against taking part in wars in which people were killed. Both strongly believed killing in wars was wrong, unethical, and immoral. Both men preferred to go to jail rather than serve in the armed forces.[22]

In 1971, however, the Supreme Court refused to hold that the draft unconstitutionally infringed on the religious liberty of those opposed to a particular war. In *Gillette* v. *United States*, the Justices ruled that fairness would be threatened by the difficulty of separating sincere conscientious objectors from false claimants.[23]

In early 1966, with the war in Vietnam growing, Muhammad Ali became eligible for the draft. On February 14, his attorney appeared before local Board 47 in Louisville, Kentucky, to present a letter requesting deferment from military service. Three days later, the request was denied. Ali was classified 1-A, eligible for military service.

All over the country people were wondering what Ali's response would be to a draft call.[24] Would he accept induction? Would he refuse to serve on the grounds of conscientious objection? Would he risk the contempt of his countrymen and go to jail?

3

Ali's Road to the Supreme Court

"Cassius Clay—Army" Lieutenant Dunkley shouted. "Cassius Clay! Will you please step forward and be inducted into the Armed Forces of the United States?"[1]

Ali remained still. He knew what the consequences were if he refused induction: five years in prison and a ten thousand dollar fine. Yet he still remained silent. He refused to serve in the Army because his religion, that of the Nation of Islam, forbade participation in war of any form. "All I did was stand up for what I believed, "Ali said later, ". . . [W]hen the time came for me to make up my mind about going in the Army, I knew people were dying in Vietnam for nothing . . . I did what was right for me."[2] Ali signed a statement

ORDER FOR TRANSFERRED MAN TO REPORT FOR INDUCTION

FROM: The President of the United States
TO: Mr. Cassius Marcellus Clay, Jr.
AKA Muhammad Ali
5962 Ardmore Street
Houston, Texas 77021

Greetings:

Having heretofore been ordered to report for induction by Local Board No. 47. State of Kentucky, Louisville, Kentucky, which is your Local Board of origin, and having been transferred upon your own request to Local Board No. 61, State of Texas, Houston, Texas, which is your Local Board of Transfer for delivery to an induction station, you will therefore report to the last named Local Board at 3rd Floor, 701 San Jacinto St., Houston, Texas 77022 on April 28, 1967, at 8:30 A.M.[3]

giving his reasons for refusing induction. He then entered the media room and handed out copies of a four-page statement, which read in part:

> My decision is a private and individual one. In taking it, I am dependent solely upon Allah as the final judge . . . . [M]any newspapers have given . . . the world the impression that . . . either I go to jail or go to the army. There is another alternative . . . justice. In the end, I am confident that . . . the truth must . . . prevail.[4]

Muhammad Ali faced the country with his principles in 1967. One hour after he refused induction, the New York State Athletic Commission suspended his boxing license; he was no longer the Heavyweight Champion of the World. It would take more than four years to get his license back, but for now, the title he had worked for was gone.

Ali flew out of Houston. From 1968 to 1970, he went into voluntary exile because he refused to serve in the Army. Ali felt strong as long as he had the support of his leader, the Honorable Elijah Muhammad.[5] Then came a new test for Ali. Elijah Muhammad banished him from the Nation of Islam. ". . . [W]e, the Muslims," he said, "are not with Ali in the desire to work in the sport for the sake of money."[6]

Ali, faced with having to support a family, had to find other means. His principal occupation, boxing, had been denied him. He never became bitter. He

Muhammad Ali bends down to pick up the envelope which contained his prepared statement explaining his refusal to accept military service.

assumed a cheerful attitude. He hoped that one day he would be welcomed back to the Nation of Islam. His savings would go towards the huge expense of carrying his case all the way to the Supreme Court.

During his exile, Muhammad Ali grew larger than sports to become a political and social force. Although there were differences among them, Ali owed particular debts to Joe Louis and Jack Johnson, who were also African-American fighters. Joe Louis had been a hero in everyone's eyes. He not only fought but he also had beaten white opponents. He basically supported the system. Louis constantly reassured whites that he was not a threat. Publicly he was an "unassuming, [G]od-fearing, mother-loving, [B]ible-reading guy."[7]

The press pictured Joe Louis as a model citizen. He entered the segregated army—whites and blacks served in separate groups in World War II. The United States Government looked to him to boost African-American troop morale. If his country's decision was to go to Vietnam, he supported that decision. Joe Louis felt that Ali did not support the country in a way he should have.[8] Even with Ali's religious beliefs, Louis thought that he should have gone into the Army in a noncombat role.[9]

Joe Louis joined the United States Army in 1942. He was a physical training instructor, and he entertained

49

soldiers with exhibitions in American and British camps. Louis, known as the Brown Bomber, was the second-ever African-American Heavyweight Champion of the World, from 1937 to 1950. Louis felt that the heavyweight champion should be the champion of all people. He has responsibilities to all people, he said.[10] Joe Louis died in 1981.

Boxer Jack Johnson's impact on African Americans was enormous. Johnson shattered the myth of white physical superiority. He had incredible talent, loved the high life, and won a lot of attention. He was the first great African-American heavyweight champion of the twentieth century. Johnson, the heavyweight champion from 1907 to 1915, was the first African-American to win the heavyweight title. For many blacks, he stood for the idea that their place was greater than the white man told them it was. Johnson was thought to be a forerunner of the new African American who emerged during World War I. African Americans became more assertive, less subservient, and more willing to defend themselves. When his boxing career began, African-American boxers were usually tolerated in America only if they were beaten. When they became dangerous, white boxers drew what was called the color line and they forced blacks to fight each other. Johnson developed exceptional defensive techniques to survive against more experienced white rivals. He lost his title in 1915 to Jess Willard. His career was put in jeopardy when he was charged with transporting a white woman for immoral purposes. Found guilty and faced with a year in prison, Johnson fled to Europe into exile. He eventually served his prison sentence. He retired from boxing altogether in 1924. Johnson died in 1946.

Ali's grandfather had once recounted an anecdote about Johnson to his grandson. "Johnson, driving one of the long, sleek, fast cars he favored, was flagged down by a country sheriff as he roared through Kentucky. He asked how much the fine was, fifty dollars he was told. He pulled off two fifties ($100) and handed them to the surprised sheriff. I'm coming back," Johnson explained.[11]

Ali's case was argued before the United States Court of Appeals for the Fifth Circuit in May 1968, and was decided a month later. Ali filed suit in the United States District Court for the Western District of Kentucky, his home state. He wanted to prevent his induction into the Army. He also wanted to prove that the Universal Military Training and Service Act was unconstitutional because of "systematic exclusion of Negroes from membership on draft boards and to restrain all draft boards in Kentucky from functioning until Negroes were appointed to boards in proportion to their ratio to the population."[12]

The District Court held that Ali had not been deprived of any right of appeal, that there was no evidence that he had been singled out or been discriminated against by the Selective Service System just because he was an African American.

Ali went on to file a similar suit in the United States District Court, Southern District of Texas. He raised the same legal issues as those raised in Kentucky. District Court Judge Hannay ruled against Ali. Then Ali appealed, to no avail.

After refusing induction on April 28, 1967, Ali filed another suit in Texas on May 1. This was also denied. The main questions to be answered were:

1. Was the Selective Service induction order invalid because of alleged systematic exclusion of African Americans from draft boards?

2. Did the District Court make a mistake in refusing to grant Ali's request for the production of certain documentary and other evidence?

3. Was there a basis of the denial of Ali of a ministerial exemption?

4. Was there a basis for the denial to Ali of conscientious objector status?[13]

According to a Selective Service report in the state of Kentucky, only 0.2 percent of 441 local board members was made up of African Americans, though 7.1 percent of the total population was African American. In Texas, only 1.1 percent of local board members was made up of African Americans, though 12.4 percent of the population was African American.[14] Not only was there an imbalance in Kentucky and Texas, it was nationwide, except for Delaware and the District of Columbia, where there was a substantial number of African-American board members.

The Selective Service regulations provide,

> In classifying a registrant there shall be no discrimination for or against him because of his race, creed, or color, or because of his membership or activity in any labor, political, religious, or other organization. Each such registrant shall receive equal justice.[15]

It cannot be denied that being drafted can deprive a person of his or her liberty and may even result in loss of life. The government argued, on the other hand, that it is the willingness of Americans to sacrifice their lives in the military service of their country that has made it possible to establish the United States as a free nation. President Lyndon Johnson said on March 6, 1967, "The knowledge that military service must sometimes be borne by—and imposed on—free men so their freedom may be preserved is woven deeply into the fabric of the American experience."[16]

All of Muhammad Ali's contentions were given conclusive consideration by a Presidential Appeal Board that was entirely independent of the director of Selective Service. The decision remained the same—that Ali be classified 1-A, thereby making him available for induction into the Army. His refusal to be inducted was sufficient for conviction.

Muhammad Ali also claimed that he was a minister of the Nation of Islam (Black Muslims) and that because of this, he was entitled to a ministerial exemption. Was he a preacher and teacher of his religious principles in a church, or did he teach and preach only occasionally? Was Ali recognized as a minister in a congregation or was he considered a leader of a group of lesser members of his faith?

Ali was certified as a minister by the national secretary of the Nation of Islam and its leader, Elijah Muhammad. He contended that he spent 90 percent of his time on his duties as a Muslim minister. He even submitted signatures of more than three thousand people who testified to his ministerial activities.

Ali's file clearly indicated that he had joined the Nation of Islam in January 1963. He had earned his living as a professional boxer and had become

Black Muslim leader Elijah Muhammad Poole (right) appears to be in deep thought as Muhammad Ali addresses a crowd at the Black Muslim Annual Convention.

Heavyweight Boxing Champion of the World on February 25, 1964. Four years earlier, he had won the light heavyweight boxing gold medal at the Rome Olympics. Shortly after returning home to a hero's welcome in Louisville, he was refused service in a restaurant because he was an African American. It has been said that he then threw his Olympic gold medal down to the bottom of the Ohio River in disgust at the country he had represented at the games.[17]

On his Selective Service forms, he listed his usual occupation as "professional boxer" and "professional prizefighter." On February 17, 1966, his 1-Y classification was changed by the local draft board to 1-A. Ali had never claimed to be a resister or conscientious objector up to that time. February 14, 1966, three days before his reclassification, he wrote to his local board, "My occupation is professional boxer and I am at present the Heavyweight Champion of the World."[18]

When he filled out the special conscientious objector form on February 28, though he claimed to be a member of the Nation of Islam, he did not claim to be a minister. When he appeared in person before his local board in March 1966, boxing was listed as his livelihood. The evidence the local board had before it was more than necessary to support Ali's 1-A classification and denial of the ministerial exemption.

On April 16, Ali wrote a long letter to the local board protesting that two years of military service would "cause him serious financial loss in being unable to pursue his livelihood as a professional boxer."[19] He went on to state:

> I am a devout Muslim and a follower of [the] Islamic religious faith under the discipline of the prophet Elijah Muhammad. To bear arms or kill is against my religion and I conscientiously object to any combat military service that involves the participation in any war in which the lives of human beings are taken.[20]

The Justice Department opposed Ali's conscientious objector claim, however. It recommended to the Appeal Board that it not be sustained. They came to the conclusion that Ali's objections to participation in war rested on primarily political and racial grounds. The Justice Department recommended that the Kentucky Appeal Board reaffirm Ali's 1-A classification.

The press raged in the aftermath of Ali's refusal to accept induction into the Army: "[Ali] seems to have gone past the borders of faith. He has reached the boundaries of fanaticism."[21] "I do not want my three boys to grow into their teens holding the belief that [Muhammad Ali] is any kind of hero . . ."[22] "There are draft-dodgers in every war, and [Muhammad Ali] isn't the only slacker in this one."[23]

On June 19, 1967, Ali's federal trial for refusing

A dejected Muhammad Ali leaves Federal Court after a federal judge tossed out the heavyweight champion's last legal effort to stay out of the U.S. Army. The champ would now be inducted or face prosecution by the Justice Department.

induction began with Judge Joe Ingraham presiding. Most of the government's case was presented by African-American Assistant United States Attorney Carl Walker. The evidence was presented the following day at 9:00 A.M. to a jury of six men and six women. First, three government officers from the Houston induction station testified about the events of April 28. The defense then called two clerks from the local board in Louisville. They testified about the racial makeup of the board. Prosecuting attorney Walker argued that there was a feeling that if Ali were allowed to escape the draft it would encourage other young men to join the Muslims.[24] At the end of the day, at ten minutes to six, the case went to the jury. A short twenty minutes later, the jurors found Ali guilty. Judge Ingraham ordered that Ali's passport be confiscated, imposed a fine of $10,000, and the maximum jail sentence: five years imprisonment. The court's action would end Ali's career in boxing; he was barred from boxing in all fifty states. But Ali never went to prison. Ali's lawyer Robert Arum began to appeal the conviction of draft evasion through the court system. During this period of appeal, Ali remained free on bail. Ali remained convinced that "someday the righteousness of his beliefs would prevail."[25] He drew on the teachings of the Nation of Islam. He never gave in to despair.

Arum was confident that Ali would win a ruling

against the Houston Federal Court's decision. The first appeal court to rule on Ali's case was the Federal Court of Appeals in New Orleans, Louisiana. That court was recognized as a fairly liberal court at that time. The New Orleans court ruled against Ali. Arum, therefore, had no other choice: if he wanted to appeal Ali's case at a higher level, he would have to take it to the country's highest legal forum, the United States Supreme Court.

Letters to Ali from all over the world poured in. One day in June of 1967, Ali met with a group of prominent African-American athletes who wanted to question him about his stand on the draft. Among them were basketball great Kareem Abdul-Jabbar and Jim Brown, football star of the Cleveland Browns. After listening to Ali, Brown and his colleagues announced to the press that they found him sincere in his beliefs.

Meanwhile, Ali discovered that there was money to be made lecturing on his view of life, and he began to appear regularly on college campuses around the country. He spoke about themes that were important to him. About the war in Vietnam he said:

> . . . I'm going to fight it legally, and if I lose, I'm just going to jail. Whatever the punishment, whatever the persecution is for standing up for my beliefs, even if it means facing machine-gun fire that day. I'll face it before denouncing Elijah Muhammad and the religion of Islam.[26]

Questions kept coming up: "Are you really sincere about standing up to jail?" "Will you back down when all the appeals are over and lost?" "Will you really serve a jail sentence?" A lawyer Ali knew in Philadelphia had followed his case closely. He suggested that there was still room for him to make some kind of agreement. Ali said no.

> . . . [I]f I was the kind of conscientious objector who can go into the armed services and do boxing exhibitions on army posts or in Vietnam or travel the country at the expense of the Government, live an easy life and be guaranteed that I won't have to get out in the mud and fight and shoot. . . . I know my image with the American public is completely ruined because of the stand I take. . . . I do it only because I mean it. I will not participate in this war.[27]

He became a hero to those rebellious youths who also refused to be drafted into the military. At the same time, each of his public appearances was monitored. A typical report by the United States Army Intelligence and Security Command read in part:

> He [Ali] arrived in . . . St. Louis to attend a Black Muslim convention. About [six hundred] persons were in attendance. [Ali] spoke for about [forty-five] minutes, mostly about . . . his cause, which is to avoid being placed in a white man's army. . . .[28]

> . . . Ali is an admitted active member of the Nation of Islam . . . a highly secretive organization . . . made up entirely of selected Negroes who . . . believe in the ultimate destruction of the white race . . . hold highly

secretive meetings which exclude all persons not
Negro, which excludes members of the news media
and which generally exclude all non-Muslims. . . .
Muslims . . . advocate that their members not serve in
the military service of our country. . . ."[29]

Then the government's case became temporarily
derailed. It was revealed that FBI agents had secretly
monitored five of Ali's phone conversations, but the
Court of Appeals ruled that the wiretaps had "resulted
in no prejudice and had no bearing on [the] defendant's
conviction."[30]

Ali showed little feeling after each setback in the
courts. "I'm being tested by Allah. I'm giving my title,
my wealth, maybe my future. Many great men have
been tested for their religious belief. If I pass this test,
I'll come out stronger than ever."[31]

He began to review his assets. Now that his boxing
career was about to end, if he were forced to retire, any
income he had would be wiped out by what he owed.
This included $250,000 in legal fees, the result of
many years of court struggles.

As the years 1969 and 1970 passed, Ali's professional status was restored. On September 28, 1970,
Federal Judge Walter Mansfield in New York authorized
renewal of Ali's boxing license in that state. Mansfield
said Ali had been denied his rights under the
Fourteenth Amendment of the Constitution, which

provides equal protection under the law.[32] Convicted robbers, rapists, and even army deserters held licenses to fight in New York State. Judge Mansfield concluded, "If those criminals were considered moral enough to box, why should Ali be singled out for conduct detrimental to the sport?"[33]

Some Muslims abandoned Ali when Elijah Muhammad disowned him, but Ali's affection for Muhammad never dimmed, nor did his fierce beliefs in the Muslim teachings ever wane. Elijah Muhammad did not want Ali to go into the Army, because he believed that war was wrong, but Ali made up his own mind. Nobody was going to put pressure on Ali to go into the Army. The final decision was all his own. He had a belief and he stuck to it.

4

The Supreme Court Deliberates

As a last resort, Ali appealed to the Supreme Court. If the Supreme Court upheld the conviction as well, then he would most certainly go to jail. On April 19, 1971, two men stood before the United States Supreme Court to begin oral arguments. One was Erwin N. Griswold, Solicitor General of the United States; the other was Chauncey Eskridge of Chicago, Illinois. He was one of several attorneys who had represented Ali in his draft litigation over the years. Four years had passed since Ali's refusal to step forward in Houston. Griswold pointed out that Ali had left little doubt when he said, "If the Vietcong were attacking his people, the Muslims would become involved in that war. . . . We [Muslims]

Muhammad Ali is led out of the Armed Forces Examining and Entrance Station after refusing Army induction. His refusal led to a legal battle for Ali that would not be resolved until the Supreme Court's decision of June 28, 1971.

don't go to war unless they are declared by Allah himself. . . ."[1] Since Ali would participate in a holy war, Griswold claimed Ali was not really a conscientious objector.

On Friday, April 23, the Supreme Court Justices in conference (a private meeting of the Supreme Court Justices that takes place periodically, usually weekly, to review new cases), at first decided, five to three, to agree with Griswold. Ali was not really a conscientious objector, and he should go to jail.

In opposing Ali's request for conscientious objector status, the Justice Department had initially advised the draft appeal board that in its view Ali failed to meet any of the three basic tests: he must show he is conscientiously opposed to war in any form, that his opposition is based upon "religious training and belief" as the term has been interpreted in former Supreme Court decisions, and he must show that this objection is sincere.[2] In arguing before the Supreme Court, the government had conceded the second and third requirements and based its case solely on the claim that because Ali would fight in a Muslim holy war, he was not opposed to war in any form.

In applying these tests, the Selective Service was expected to concern itself with the individual and not with its own interpretation of the beliefs of the religious sect, if any, to which he belonged. Selective Service officials were led to believe that the Justice Department had found that Ali had failed to satisfy each of the three basic tests for qualification as a conscientious objector. As to the requirement that a registrant must be opposed to war in any form, a long letter of explanation from the Department said that Ali's beliefs "do not appear to preclude military service in any form, but rather are limited to military service in the Armed Forces of the United States. . . . These constitute only objections to certain types of war in certain circumstances."[3] The Justice Department said that Ali had not consistently manifested his conscientious objector claim. Its letter went on to say:

> It seems clear that the teachings of the Nation of Islam preclude fighting for the Untied States not because of objections to participation in war in any form but rather because of political and racial objections to policies of the United States as interpreted by Elijah Muhammad. . . . It is therefore our conclusion that registrant's claimed objections to participation in war insofar as they are based upon the teaching of the Nation of Islam, rest on grounds which are primarily political and racial.[4]

As to the requirement that a registrant's opposition to war must be sincere, that part of the letter began: "The registrant had not consistently manifested his conscientious objector claim and had not shown overt manifestations sufficient to establish his subjective belief where his claim was not asserted until military service became imminent."[5]

The Justice Department should not have advised Ali's draft board to disregard the finding "the registrant is sincere in his objection" simply because of the circumstance and timing of Ali's claim. Since the Appeal Board gave no reasons for its denial of Ali's claim, there is no way of knowing on which of the three grounds it relied. The Justice Department also had mistakenly advised the Board that Ali's beliefs were not religiously based and were not sincerely held.[6]

There were many people who believed that, despite the change of mood in the country, Ali belonged in jail. On March 30, 1971, Congressman George Andrews of Alabama addressed the House of Representatives:

> I . . . thought about . . . one Cassius Clay, alias Muhammad Ali, who several years ago defied the U.S. Government, thumbed his nose at the flag, and is still walking the streets making millions of dollars fighting for pay, not for his country. . . . Where on earth is the Justice Department in this country? Why on earth is not that man Cassius Clay in the penitentiary where he should be?[7]

When the case, *Clay* v. *United States*, came before the Supreme Court in 1971, Associate Justice William J. Brennan, Jr., appointed to the Supreme Court by

President Dwight D. Eisenhower in 1956, was the only Justice who wanted to hear it.[8] Apart from war and draft issues, the case had racial overtones as well. After all, Ali was one of the country's most popular African-American athletes. Few defendants ever have their case reach the Supreme Court for review, but Ali was well-known. A judgment against him could spark great controversy.

Appeals had taken six years. Ali had been banned from boxing for nearly four. Public sympathy began to grow for Ali. The case had come before the Supreme Court two terms earlier. The Justices, in conference had voted not to hear it. Ali's conviction stood. The government, however, made a last-minute disclosure that Ali had been overheard on a national security wiretap. This prevented the announcement of the Supreme Court's decision. This technically allowed the Supreme Court to send the case back to a lower court for more hearings. The Justices had hoped it would not surface again.[9] When it did, however, it was Justice Brennan who would persuade the others to hear the case.

Thurgood Marshall recused himself (he removed himself from participation to avoid a conflict of interest). He had been Solicitor General of the United States for two years when the case began in early 1967. The Solicitor General is the third ranking member of the

The members of the Supreme Court during *Clay* v. *United States*. Top row, left to right: Thurgood Marshall, Potter Stewart, Byron White, and Harry Blackmun. The bottom row, left to right: John Harlan, Hugo Black, Chief Justice Warren Burger, William Douglas, and William Brennan.

Justice Department behind the Attorney General. Many appeals come across the desk of the Solicitor General. His or her job is to decide which appeals should be presented before the Supreme Court. He or she handles the briefing and argument of those appeals before the Supreme Court. The Justices rely heavily on the Solicitor General to help choose and present the most pressing cases for review. The Court grants approximately 80 percent of the petitions submitted by the Solicitor General as opposed to only about 3 percent submitted by other lawyers across the country.[10] Thurgood Marshall was one of the four solicitors general who later served on the Supreme Court. Marshall was appointed to the Court by President Lyndon Johnson and was sworn in August 24, 1967, to become the first African-American Justice on the United States Supreme Court.

Chief Justice Warren Burger assigned Associate Justice John Marshall Harlan to write the majority opinion and Harlan's law clerks began preparing the draft opinion. One of his clerks had read one of the most trusted texts of the Black Muslims, *Message to the Blackman* [sic] *in America*, written by Elijah Muhammad. Both clerks became convinced that Ali's willingness to fight in a holy war was not relevant.[11] For all practical purposes, Ali was opposed to all wars.

Harlan's first inclination was not to buy any of this. He agreed, however, to take his clerks' background material. He would study it at his home in Georgetown. The following morning, after reading all of the material, he surprised his clerks. He agreed wholeheartedly and asked that the material be incorporated, as written, into the draft opinion.[12] Harlan had been persuaded that the United States government, despite the Justice Department's finding that Ali was sincerely opposed to all wars, had misinterpreted the Black Muslim Doctrine, which said:

> The very dominant idea in Islam is the making of peace and not war; our refusing to go armed is our proof that we want peace. We felt that we had no right to take part in a war with nonbelievers of Islam who have always denied us justice and equal rights; and if we were going to be examples of peace and righteousness (as Allah has chosen us to be) we felt we had no right to join hands with the murderers of people or to help murder those who have done us no wrong.[13]

Harlan wanted to confront the Justice Department's misrepresentation.[14] There was no basis in fact, all along, for the claim that Ali was not really opposed to all shooting wars.[15]

There had been no indication outside his chambers that Harlan's view had changed. When his memo to the other Justices circulated suggesting a reversal of Ali's conviction, the Court exploded. Chief Justice Warren

Muhammad Ali carries religious books into the Federal Building. After studying the foundations of Ali's beliefs, Justice Harlan changed his vote to favor Ali.

Burger was upset. How could Harlan change sides without notifying him? He was even more irritated by the inclusion of the Black Muslim Doctrine in the draft opinion. Chief Justice Burger told one law clerk that Harlan had become an "apologist for the Black Muslims."[16]

John Harlan shifted his vote in favor of Ali to even the balance at four and four. This meant, however, that Ali would still go to jail. Seventy-two year old Justice Harlan who had served on the Court since 1955, was dying of cancer. He eventually resigned. He died in December 1971. Chief Justice Burger was not going to shift his own vote; nor were Associate Justices Hugo Black, Byron White, and Harry Blackmun. They were disturbed that Harlan wanted to emphasize the United States government's twisting of the facts. Harlan's opinion could mean that "all Black Muslims would be eligible for the conscientious objector status."[17] The 1970–1971 Court term was coming to a close. If the Court stayed deadlocked, Ali would surely go to jail for draft evasion. In addition, since decisions in which the Justices were equally divided were generally not accompanied by opinions, Ali would never know why he had lost.

Associate Justice Potter Stewart suggested an alternative. The Court could set Ali free by citing a technical error by the Justice Department.[18] Stewart's proposal had several advantages: the ruling in this case would not become a precedent—in other words it would not serve as an example for other rulings of a similar nature. It also would not broaden the categories under which others might claim to be conscientious objectors.

The Supreme Court reversed Ali's conviction in the Federal District Court for the Southern District of Texas and the Federal Court of Appeals for the Fifth Circuit for refusal to submit to induction. Six members of the Court (Justices Stewart, Burger, Black, White, Blackmun, and Brennan) expressed the view that: since the registrant's (Ali) beliefs were founded on the tenets of the Muslim religion as he understands them, they were religiously based and therefore satisfied the test for qualification as a conscientious objector; since the hearing officer found that Ali was sincere in his objections, and thus met another test for qualification as a conscientious objector, the Justice Department erred in advising the Kentucky Appeal Board to disregard this finding simply because he did not assert his claim until military service became imminent; whether or not Ali met the third test of conscientious objection to war in any form, it was not clear that the Kentucky Appeal

Board relied on some legitimate ground in denying the claim. Therefore the conviction could not stand.

In separate opinions, Justice Douglas concurred on the ground that the First Amendment freedom of religion clause precluded Ali's induction, since in accordance with the Koran, he believed only in religious wars against nonbelievers.

Justice Harlan concurred on the ground that the Kentucky Appeal Board might have acted on the Justice Department's incorrect advice that Ali's proof of sincerity was insufficient as a matter of law because his claim had not been timely asserted. Justice Marshall did not participate.[19]

Justice Stewart said that the Board of Appeals had never indicated the actual basis on which Ali's request for conscientious objector status had been denied. He argued that it was possible, in theory, that the denial was based on findings that Ali's position was not sincerely held or that it was not based upon religious training and belief. The United States Government now conceded that these positions were wrong.

Chief Justice Burger at first refused to go along with Stewart's proposal. Ali now had seven votes. That left Burger with a problem: if he dissented, it might seem like a racist vote. Eventually he came around to agreeing with Stewart's logic. He decided to join the other

Justices in an 8-0 decision (Thurgood Marshall not voting) in favor of Ali.

Ali's victory was announced on June 28, 1971. He never realized just how close he had come to going to jail. "I thank Allah," he said, when he heard the good news in Chicago, "and I thank the Supreme Court for recognizing the sincerity of the religious teachings that I've accepted."[20]

The process through the courts had lasted forty-eight months to the day. Ali had refused induction on June 28, 1967. All criminal charges against him were now dismissed.

The Supreme Court, however, could not give him back his title. He had to do that himself in the boxing ring. On October 30, 1974, Muhammad Ali knocked out George Foreman in eight rounds to regain the title of Heavyweight Champion of the World.

5

Aftermath

On the morning of June 28, 1971, Ali was driving around Chicago's South Side when he stopped at an orange juice stand. He stepped out of the car. A man came running toward him. "I just heard it on the radio," he shouted, "the Supreme Court said you're free."[1]

The Court had decided that Ali's religious convictions were sincere. Ali was a free man. At a time when the country was being torn apart, when the government was lying to its people, Ali was speaking the truth as he saw it.[2] By this time, Ali, who turned twenty-nine in 1971, had passed the draft's age limit of twenty-six. He could no longer be drafted so he would not need to be reclassified.

Ali bore no grudges against those who had wronged

him. "They only did what was right at the time," he declared, "I did what I thought was right. . . . I can't condemn them. . . ."[3] Ali confided to sportscaster Howard Cosell, "The Supreme Court decision is a load off my mind."[4] It was back to boxing.

Ali had good reasons for keeping his conversion to the Nation of Islam a secret in the 1960s when racial tensions in the United States were reaching a breaking point. As civil right groups pressed for racial justice and equality in the South, their demands were officially met by attacks from the police. The black sections of most large cities were seething with tension.

It was a time of violence and assassination. Robert Kennedy and Martin Luther King, Jr., were both killed by assassins' bullets in 1968. Some people in the United States hated Ali. But he never stopped moving freely in public. "God is my bodyguard. Allah watches over me. . . . Allah fixes the time when all of us will be taken."[5]

The case of *Clay* v. *United States* was processed at a time in this country when people were clamoring for law and order. The decade of the 1970s was closing with a kind of moral fatigue, a sense of despair and futility. Nearly every manner of protest had been deployed over Vietnam—bombings, petitions, demonstrations—but the fighting continued. A significant change was occurring. America was turning against the war in Vietnam. The country was tired of ritual body counts from Saigon. Many activists stopped protesting. The civil rights movement seemed to be over. The only thing that went on uninterrupted was the Vietnam War. As the Nixon Administration negotiated agreements for the easing of tensions with China and the former Soviet Union, the Vietnam War ceased to threaten as an international crisis.

A total military withdrawal was in the country's best interests. While Vietnam waned as an international crisis, it intensified as an institutional issue that focused on the Nixon presidency. By the fall of 1971 (three months after the *Clay* decision by the Supreme Court), polls suggested that popular confidence in American leaders had declined, and opposition to the Vietnam War was greater than at any time in the 1960s.[6]

The Nixon Administration continued to remove American troops from Vietnam in early 1971. On April 7, Nixon announced the withdrawal of another hundred thousand troops by December.

The World Boxing Association (WBA) and other fight authorities began, in July 1971, to restore Ali to the ranks of the officially recognized, but none offered an apology. When asked if he would sue to recover some of the money he would have made in the boxing ring

After the Supreme Court decision, Muhammad Ali could once again focus solely on his boxing career.

during his three-and-a-half year exile, Ali said no; nobody could give him back those years that had been taken from him.

Ali began his climb back to the top of the boxing world. He did not want to be put into retirement. He fought Ken Norton and Joe Frazier in matches and rematches. In 1974, Ali made a trip to Africa, the continent of his ancestors. Ali had always taken great pride in his African ancestry and always encouraged other African Americans to do the same. Ali beat George Foreman there to become the second boxer ever to win the heavyweight title twice (Floyd Patterson was the first). Ali had regained the title that had been taken away from him in 1967. He was a champion again, and he could enjoy the privileges of being at the top.

When Ali became a Muslim, he told the world, "I don't have to be what you want me to be. I'm free to be what I want."[7] When asked how he would celebrate his Supreme Court victory, Ali replied, "I've already said a long prayer to Allah, that's my celebration."[8]

State governments, veterans' groups and others suggested that Ali leave the country. If he were to remain a sports hero in the United States, it might encourage other young people to avoid their patriotic duty. Those who had kept Ali from boxing in the United States relented, however, and the door was reopened. He fought and won three more bouts. Ali gained allies in African-American leaders Dr. Martin Luther King Jr., New York Congressman Adam Clayton Powell, and Georgia legislator Julian Bond. To them, Ali was an example of "black manhood standing tall against an illegal and immoral system."[9]

On December 10, 1974, Muhammad Ali visited the White House to talk with President Gerald R. Ford. "I accepted his decision," said President Ford, ". . . I firmly believe that as time goes on, Muhammad Ali will be remembered for more than just excellence in athletics."[10]

Ali's victory over Foreman lifted spirits around the world. Past hatreds had been forgotten. Longtime detractors became friends. Ali was named *Ring* magazine's Fighter of the Year and *Sports Illustrated* called him Sportsman of the Year.

Perhaps a well-known sportswriter put it best when he wrote:

> There are certain heroes of sports who transcend the games. . . . Muhammad Ali does it best of all. It is time to recognize Ali for what he is . . . one of the most important and brave men of all American time. The time has come to end the bitterness and forget the past. . . .[11]

The country that had turned away from Ali was turning back. Well-known novelist Irwin Shaw headed

Muhammad Ali regained the heavyweight championship in 1974 by beating George Foreman. Later, that year he was named *Ring* magazine's Fighter of the Year.

a group of editors and writers demanding Ali's reinstatement. The students and teachers he had met on the college circuit while he was in exile formed another group demanding fair play, especially after the news of the illegally gathered evidence by the Federal Bureau of Investigation through phone wiretaps.

The case was closed, and the years of uncertainty were over. Ali's lawyer Robert Arum said, "This case proves that our Justice system works . . . if you have the money and the influence to go all the way."[12] Ali had been right about the war all along, people said, but it was too late—"not only for 45,000 dead Americans, but for one live Muslim."[13]

6

Looking Into the Future

In 1973 the United States government stopped drafting people into the armed services and accepted only volunteers. The government also created a stand-by draft. This was run by the Selective Service System, a government agency. Under the stand-by draft, men who had reached the age of eighteen were required to register with the Selective Service System through local draft boards. The stand-by draft was discontinued in 1975. In 1980, however, Congress passed laws resuming registration requirements for the draft. Under the new laws, men who reached the age of nineteen or twenty in 1980 were required to register with the Selective Service System that year. Beginning in 1981, all men were required to register for the draft when they reached the age of eighteen. This registration system was designed to provide the government with a list of men who could be inducted into the armed forces in the event of a national emergency.

Today, the United States maintains volunteer military forces that offer good pay and many benefits to both men and women who enlist. This all-volunteer system tends to produce armed forces with better-trained personnel who will probably serve for longer periods. However, its disadvantages include higher costs and difficulty in attracting enough people when needed.

Many people think that military service should be an obligation of American citizenship. Also, some see the draft—and the resulting lower military pay—as a way to reduce military spending in this country. The law currently provides for different terms of conscientious objector service. The difference depends on whether or not conscientious objectors are willing to accept service in the army that does not require them to carry weapons.

Noncombatants (classified 1-A-O) serve in the army without using weapons or handling ammunition. They are not trained to use weapons. Noncombatants have usually served in the medical corps.

Conscientious objectors who are opposed to any military service are classified 1-0. When they are ordered to alternative service they are reclassified 1-W.

Many alternative service workers (ASWs) find their own jobs for approval by the Selective Service System. In the past, many conscientious objectors worked in hospitals and in programs operated by religious organizations.

People requesting conscientious objector status while in the military must request either discharge or transfer to noncombatant duty. Upon discharge, if they are subject to the draft, they will be classified 1-O-S. Those who have not completed their service obligation may be liable to alternative service for the uncompleted part of military service if they are drafted at a later time.

Other types of conscientious objectors include:

1. *Nuclear Pacifists.* Those whose consciences do not permit them to participate in a nuclear war or what they believe would become a nuclear war. Some nuclear pacifists become opposed to all war because they believe all wars fought by the major powers could lead to the use of nuclear weapons. At this time, current policy in the armed forces is to reassign those who have moral reservations about handling or firing nuclear weapons.

2. *Noncooperators.* Those who will not cooperate with the draft system. They are conscientiously opposed to participation in war and they conclude that the draft system furthers war. Many of them refuse to register for the draft. The Selective Service System does

not recognize conscientious objection to participation in the draft system even though the draft *itself* serves the purposes of war.

When Draft registration was resumed in 1980 it was meant to send a message to the Russians. The Selective Service director called it a "weapon in our arsenal like a bomber or missile."[1] Others have valued the draft because they believe it helps to prevent the enemy from attacking us. Conscientious objection is not acknowledged by the government at registration. Nor are conscientious objectors allowed to decide not to register. The maximum possible sentence for draft violators is five years in prison and a fine of $250,000. Of those convicted for not registering, most have served short sentences, been ordered to do community service, been put on probation and/or paid a fine of $10,000 or less.[2] Non registrants are denied federal aid for education and job training and are barred from most employment with the federal government.

For the draft to begin again, Congress would have to authorize it and the president would have to order it to start. A draft lottery would then be held in which everyone born in a certain year would have their birthday matched up with a lottery number. Draft registrants who turn twenty in the present calendar year would be called first, beginning with those who have

Muhammad Ali leaves the induction center in Houston, Texas, escorted by members of his entourage. Ali eventually received a legal conscientious objector exemption from the United States government.

the lowest lottery numbers. The first draftees would have only ten days before they would have to appear for a physical examination and induction.

Those who wanted conscientious objector status or other classification would notify the area Selective Service office by submitting a form before induction day. They might also be required to submit to an army physical and mental examination before their conscientious objector claims could be heard.

The conscientious objector claimant would be required to appear at a local board hearing scheduled on a ten-day notice. Up to three witnesses could speak in support of the claimant. If the claim were denied, the local board would have to tell you why and the denial could be appealed.

The United States Government has war-making powers and legal authority to draft people into the Armed Services at any time. The law also requires, however, that the government recognize conscientious objectors. It provides that during a draft, conscientious objectors can serve in tasks not directly tied to combat or they can work as civilians to serve society.

Ali received a legal conscientious objector exemption. Many others throughout history have been denied legal exemptions and were imprisoned. Draft resisters brought conscience to the courts. During the more "popular wars" (World War I and II), court decisions reflected the patriotic mood of the country. Conscientious objection was viewed as treason. Anti-war appeals to conscience fell on deaf ears.

As opposition to the Vietnam War increased, the judicial system responded with increasing flexibility. Between 1967 and 1975, the percentage of defendants convicted of Selective Service Act violations dropped every year. The average sentence of those convicted also dropped. In 1967, for instance, 75 percent of all defendants were convicted. By 1970, the conviction rate fell to just over 36 percent and by 1975, less than 17 percent of all draft law defendants were convicted.[3] In 1967, almost 90 percent of those convicted received jail sentences, by 1975, less than 9 percent went to prison.[4]

Both the drop in conviction and imprisonment rates indicate a change in judicial attitude. Draft resisters were no longer viewed as dangerous or un-American. Some judges even praised the courage of resisters. One Federal District Court judge from upstate New York called the Vietnam War "a horror" and praised the courage displayed by war resisters who had raided a local draft board.[5]

By the end of the Vietnam War both legal and illegal draft resisters had seriously undermined the ability of the Selective Service to induct large numbers of young men into the armed services. In 1970, 25 percent of all inductees were granted conscientious objector status, in 1971, more than 42 percent, toward the end of the Vietnam War in 1973, 73 percent. By 1972, more young men were exempted from the draft than were inducted into the armed services.[6]

The number of criminal defendants rose during the Vietnam War. Between 1965 and 1975 over 22,000 men were indicted for draft law violations. The overwhelming majority of those convicted were motivated by anti-war sentiments. For the first time in history, religious objectors were in the minority; only 7 percent of the convicted resisters came from traditional pacifist religions.[7]

As the Vietnam War continued, the percentage of young men willing to face prosecution also rose. By 1972, 12 percent of all inductees were indicted. A young man facing induction during the Vietnam War was one thousand times more likely to resist the draft and be indicted than in prior war conflicts.[8]

By the end of the Vietnam War the Selective Service System was demoralized. It became increasingly difficult to induct men in the Army. There was more and more illegal resistance. The draft was all but dead.

Draft registration was suspended in April 1975, twenty-one months after President Richard M. Nixon officially ended the draft. For the first time since 1948 no young men were drafted into the armed forces. The longest standing draft in American history had come to an end. In 1975, President Gerald R. Ford issued a proclamation terminating the remaining draft registration requirements. The draft was reinstated for a brief time under President Jimmy Carter in response to the Soviet's invasion of Afghanistan in 1980.

The country had turned around, the Vietnam War was discredited. The resisters were vindicated. Instead of being attacked on Capitol Hill, draft resisters were being praised. A member of the House of Representatives even thanked the resisters for helping change public opinion on the war and the draft.[9]

The resistance ended the longest draft in history and helped alter the country's policy of intervention abroad. All the tradition and tactics of war resistance came together during the Vietnam War period. Religious ideals against killing were joined with pacifist politics. War, as a foundation for American international relations, was dealt a blow.

But the movement did not put an end to militarism. The army of draftees was replaced by a volunteer army. The nuclear arms race escalated. Warfare has changed, the advent of nuclear war has given added power and appeal to the nonviolent policy of draft resistance. The possibility of a nuclear holocaust has forced new generations to reevaluate their willingness to support warfare in any capacity.

The Selective Service system today is but a shell of what it was at the height of the Vietnam War. Then, it had over eight thousand employees across the United States, more than three hundred fifty thousand men a year received draft notices. Today, there are about two hundred employees divided between an office building in Arlington, Virginia and a data-processing center just north of Chicago, Illinois.[10]

The Pentagon has said that the Clinton Administration policy of having military strong enough to fight and win two major regional conflicts at the same time could be fulfilled without reinstating the draft.[11] The Department of Defense has opposed proposals for national service citizen soldiers, preferring the present all-volunteer military.

In 1996, President Bill Clinton was entangled in controversies over his own draft record during the war in Vietnam. In 1994, Clinton commended the report from the Pentagon which conceded there was no need for draft registration. The tide of a draft, however, was maintained. Some military leaders, Senators, and civilian analysts view the draft as a way to make all social classes share in the defense of our country. Actually, only a very large draft that took most eligible men (as

Muhammad Ali retired from boxing as one of the greatest fighters of all time. His career record was 56-5, and he was the first man to win the heavyweight championship three times.

in World War II) would evenly draw from all social and ethnic groups.

Officially, the Pentagon lists 210 conscientious objector claims for 1990. There are no numbers listed at all for 1991.[12] However, military counseling agencies estimate that at least a thousand reservists and active-duty troops are restricted to their bases for refusing orders.

Resistance to the war within military ranks is widespread. Some reservists and active-duty personnel have spoken out at anti-war rallies. The smaller volume of active-duty and reserve troops refusing to serve in the Persian Gulf War in 1991 stands in dramatic contrast to the early years of Vietnam.

Military counselors and veterans attributed resistance in the ranks to changes brought on by an all-volunteer Army. Conducted polls show that half of all Americans oppose going to war.[13] The troops, like the American public, will prove reluctant to support a long ground war. Resistance within the military may turn out to be the most powerful element in the anti-war movement. Many of today's recruits are the children of Vietnam veterans with firsthand experience of that war's devastating toll on its survivors. At present, there are many allurements intended for shaping an all-volunteer army such as higher salaries and college tuition programs.

There has been a flood of recruits who want to take advantage of these incentives. Although young soldiers are willing to fight for their country, their volunteer status also means that they want to judge the cause they are being asked to die for.

Muhammad Ali, now in his fifties, lives on the Ali Farm in southwestern Michigan with his fourth wife and son. He has suffered from Parkinson's Syndrome (a chronic progressive nervous disease that is marked by tremors and muscle weakness) since 1984. Ali receives about three hundred letters a week from fans all over the world and he answers every one. He also autographs photos and considers every signature a good deed. "I'm just tryin' to get to heaven," Ali said on a recent television program. He added, "I believe it is against Islam to deceive people."[14]

Questions for Discussion

1. Muhammad Ali stood up for what he believed in, despite the fact that his beliefs were not accepted by many people. Has there ever been a time in your life when you stood up for something unpopular? Discuss what happened and how it made you feel.

2. Under current regulations, women cannot serve in ground combat troops. Discuss whether you agree or disagree with this. Support your answer.

3. Do you agree with the idea that people who have sincere religious or moral objections to war should not be required to serve in combat? Why? Why not? What kinds of alternate service, if any, would you find acceptable?

4. Many people who were eligible for the draft during the Vietnam War left the country and fled to Canada to avoid serving in the military. Do you agree or disagree with this method of avoiding service? Support your answer.

5. Do you think that the criteria that the Selective Service Board required that Muhammad Ali meet in order to be considered a conscientious objector are valid? Why? Why not?

Chapter Notes

Chapter 1

1. Muhammad Ali with Richard Durham, *The Greatest: My Own Story* (New York: Random House, 1975), p. 101
2. Thomas Hauser, *Muhammad Ali: His Life and Times* (New York: Simon & Schuster, 1991), p. 82.
3. Ibid., pp. 82–83.
4. Wilen A. Bijlefeld, "Black Muslims," *Grolier Electronic Encyclopedia Publishing, Inc.* 1995.
5. Malu Halasa, *Elijah Muhammad* (New York: Chelsea House, 1990), p. 93.
6. Ibid., p. 87.
7. Bijlefeld, "Black Muslims," *Grolier Electronic Encyclopedia Publishing, Inc.* 1995.
8. Hauser, p. 90.
9. Arnold Hano, *Muhammad Ali: The Champion*, (New York: G.P. Putnam's Sons, 1977), p. 73.
10. "Clay Puts Black Muslim X in his Name," *The New York Times*, March 7, 1964, p.15.
11. Hauser, p. 141.
12. Ibid., p. 97.
13. "Clay Says He Has Adopted Islam Religion and Regards it as Way to Peace," *The New York Times*, February 28, 1964, p. 22.
14. Hauser, p. 143.
15. Ibid., pp. 154–155.
16. 397 Federal Reports 2d 901 (Fifth Circuit, 1968).
17. *Clay* v. *United States*, 403 US 698 (1971).
18. "Rivers May Seek Change in Draft," *The New York Times*, August 26, 1966, p. 3.
19. Hauser, p. 155.
20. *Congressional Record*, February 21, 1967, p. 4134.
21. Robert H. Boyle, "Champ in the Jug?," *Sports Illustrated*, April 10, 1967, p. 30.
22. Halasa, p. 59.
23. Ali and Durham, p.162.
24. Ibid.
25. Ibid., p. 169.
26. Ibid., p. 171.
27. Ibid., p. 172

Chapter 2

1. Stephen M. Kohn, *Jailed for Peace: The History of American Draft Law Violators 1658–1985* (Westport, Conn.: Greenwood Press, 1986), p. 7.

2. "A History of Conscription in America from the Colonial Era to Vietnam," *Editorial Research Reports,* Washington, D.C.: Congressional Quarterly Inc., January 11, 1991, p. 23.

3. Henry David Thoreau, *Civil Disobedience,* ed. Philip Van Doren Stern (New York: Clarkson N. Potter Inc., 1970), p. 456.

4. Elder Witt, ed., *Congressional Quarterly's Guide to the U.S. Supreme Court*, 2nd ed., (Washington, D.C.: Congressional Quarterly Inc. 1995), p. 455.

5. "Conscientious Objectors," Washington, D.C.: *Congressional Quarterly Almanac*, 1971, p. 263.

6. *Editorial Research Reports,* p. 23.

7. *United States* v. *Macintosh* 283 US 605 (1931).

8. Thomas Conklin, *Muhammad Ali: The Fight for Respect* (Brookfield, Conn.: Millbrook Press, 1991), p. 67.

9. Ibid.

10. Jack Rummel, *Muhammad Ali* (New York: Chelsea House, 1988), p. 59.

11. Ibid.

12. Howard Cosell, *Cosell* (Chicago: Playboy Press, 1973), p. 205.

13. Joseph A. Califano, Jr., *The Triumph and Tragedy of Lyndon Johnson* (New York: Simon & Schuster, 1991), p. 250.

14. Doris Kearns, *Lyndon Johnson and the American Dream* (New York: Harper & Row, 1976), p. 349.

15. Califano, p. 272.

16. *Welsh* v. *United States*, 398 US 333, 1970.

17. *Facts on File* (New York: Facts on File, Inc., 1970, Vol XXX), p. 422.

18. *United States* v. *Seeger* 380 US 163, (1965).

19. *Welsh* v. *United States* 398 US 333, (1970).

20. The Military Selective Service Act on Conscientious Objection/Public Law 129, 92nd Congress, September 28, 1971, Section 6(j) Conscientious Objection.

21. *United States* v. *Seeger* 380 US 163, (1965).

22. *Welsh* v. *United States* 398 US 333, (1970).

23. *Gillette* v. *United States* 401 US 437, (1971).

24. Cosell, p. 199.

Chapter 3

1. Muhammad Ali with Richard Durham, *The Greatest: My Own Story* (New York: Random House, 1975), p. 156.

2. Thomas Hauser, *Muhammad Ali: His Life and Times* (New York: Simon & Schuster, 1991), p. 172.

3. Ali and Durham, p. 156.

4. Federal Bureau of Investigation Files (1968), as quoted in Hauser, p. 170.

5. Ferdie Pacheco, *Muhammad Ali: A View from the Corner* (New York: Brichlane/CarolRhoda Publishing, 1992), p. 87.

6. Ibid.

7. Hauser, p. 206

8. Ibid., p. 134.

9. Ibid., p. 206

10. Ibid., P. 133.

11. Howard Cosell, *Cosell* (Chicago: Playboy Press, 1973), pp. 204–205.

12. "Conscientious Objectors," *Congressional Quarterly Almanac* Washington, D.C.: 1971. p. 263.

13. *Welsh* v. *United States*, 398 US 333 (1970).

14. U.S. Department of Commerce, Special Consensus, p. 28, No. 1377 (1964).

15. Selective Service Regulations (32 C.F.R.), Par. 1622 1 (d).

16. Lyndon B. Johnson. *Message on Selective Service to the United States Congress*, March 6, 1967.

17. Ali and Durham, p. 59.

18. *Cassius Marsellus Clay* v. *United States of America*, United States Court of Appeals. Fifth Circuit 307 F 24, 901 (1968).

19. Letter from Muhammad Ali to Local Board No. 47, Louisville, Kentucky. April 16, 1966.

20. Ibid.

21. Hauser, p. 177.

22. Ibid.

23. Ibid.

24. Ibid., p. 180.

25. Jack Rummel, *Muhammad Ali* (New York: Chelsea House Publishers, 1988), p. 63.

26. Hauser, p. 187.

27. Ali and Durham, p. 181.

28. Federal Bureau of Investigation Files (1968).

29. Hauser, p. 191.

30. 430 Federal Reports 2d 165 (5th Circuit, 1970).

31. *Sporting News*, October 12, 1987, as quoted in Hauser, p. 193.

32. Cosell, p. 207.

33. Thomas Conklin, *Muhammad Ali: The Fight for Respect* (Brookfield, Conn.: Millbrook Press, 1991), p. 74.

Chapter 4

1. Bob Woodward and Scott Armstrong, *The Brethren Inside the Supreme Court* (New York: Simon & Schuster, 1979), p. 137.

2. Maureen Harrison and Steven Gilbert, eds., *Landmark Decisions of the United States Supreme Court* (LaJolla, Calif.: Excellent Books, 1994), p. 162.

3. Ibid.

4. *Clay v. United States* 403 US 698, (1971).

5. Ibid.

6. Harrison and Gilbert, p. 165.

7. *Congressional Record*. March 30, 1971. p. 8630. (Proceedings and debates of the 92nd Congress). Vol. 117, Part 7, Washington, D.C.: U.S. Government Printing Office, 1971.

8. Woodward and Armstrong, p. 136.

9. Ibid., p. 137.

10. Kermit L. Hall, ed., *The Oxford Companion to the Supreme Court of the United States* (New York: Oxford University Press, 1992), p. 803.

11. Woodward and Armstrong, p. 137.

12. Ibid.

13. Elijah Muhammad, *Message to the Blackman in America* (Newport News, Virg.: United Brothers Communications Systems, 1992), p. 322.

14. Woodward and Armstrong, p. 138.

15. Ibid.

16. Ibid.

17. Ibid.

18. Ibid.

19. *Clay v. United States* 403 US 698, (1971).

20. Woodward and Armstrong, pp. 138–139.

Chapter 5

1. Robert Lipsyte, *Free to be Muhammad Ali* (New York: Harper & Row Publishers, 1979), p. 98.

2. Thomas Hauser, *Muhammad Ali: His Life and Times* (New York: Simon & Schuster, 1991), p. 199.

3. "Don't Call Me Champ," *The Nation,* July 19, 1971. p. 34.

4. Howard Cosell, *Cosell* (Chicago: Playboy Press, 1973), p. 219.

5. Hauser, p. 287.

6. *The New York Times*, November 5, 1971. Section 1, p. 48.

7. "Don't Call Me Champ," *The Nation,* July 19, 1971. p. 36.

8. "Decision for Allah," *Newsweek,* July 12, 1971. p. 61.

9. Lipsyte, p. 77.

10. Hauser, p. 282.

11. Ibid., pp. 280-281.

12. Lipsyte, p. 99.

13. Arnold Hano, *Muhammad Ali the Champion* (New York: G.P. Putnam's Sons, 1977), p. 99.

Chapter 6

1. "Who is a Conscientious Objector?" *National Interreligious Service Board for Conscientious Objectors (NISBCO)* pamphlet. Washington, D.C., 1995. p. 6.

2. Ibid., p. 7.

3. Stephen M. Kohn, *Jailed for Peace* (Westport, Conn.: Greenwood Press, 1986), p. 89.

4. Ibid.

5. Ibid., p. 90.

6. Selective Service System, Conscientious Objectors Special Monograph, No. 11, 53, 214–215 as shown in Table 7, Kohn p. 93.

7. Kohn, p. 93.

8. Ibid.

9. Ibid., p. 94.

10. David E. Rosenbaum, "The Republicans Are Threatening to Bury the Ghost of the Military Draft," *The New York Times,* July 16, 1995. pp. 16–17.

11. NISBCO, p. 3.

12. Rosenbaum, p. 17.

13. Bruce Shapiro, "Hell For Those Who Won't Go," *The Nation,* February 18, 1991. p. 194.

14. CBS-TV Interview with Ed Bradley on *60 Minutes*, March 17, 1996.

Glossary

1-A classification—Status indicating eligibility for unrestricted military service.

abolitionist—One who is opposed to slavery.

amendment—Measure added to the United States Constitution since it was adopted in 1787. The first ten amendments are known as the Bill of Rights.

claimant—Someone who submits a claim to the Selective Service System to qualify for a classification other than "available for military service."

colonialism—Control by one power over a dependent area or people.

Communism—A system of government in which a single authoritarian party controls state-owned means of production, where goods are owned in common and are available to all as needed.

conscientious objector—One who is conscientiously opposed to war in any form, and whose opposition is based upon religious training and belief.

conscription—Process of requiring an individual to serve in the military for a specified period. Common term: the Draft.

draft law—Set of statutes passed by Congress. The regulations and the decisions in court cases interpreting them that together govern both how the government is supposed to act and how people subject to its authority are to act.

Federal Bureau of Investigation (FBI)—Investigative branch of United States Department of Justice established in 1908.

heavyweight—Boxing classification of someone who is above average in weight in an unlimited weight division. Muhammad Ali was World Heavyweight Champion 1964–1967; 1974–1978; 1978–1979.

Islam—Major world religion founded by the prophet Muhammad in seventh century A.D. Today, there are about 600 million Muslims.

Military Selective Service Act—Last revised and enacted in 1971 and amended since then, it defines the United States government's authority to draft people.

moral and ethical beliefs—Beliefs about right and wrong, and good and bad behavior. The Supreme Court has decided that these beliefs qualify as a basis for conscientious objection.

mosque—Muslim place of worship.

Muslims—People who believe in the religion of Islam. Literally "ones who submit."

Nation of Islam—Based on beliefs of traditional Islam with a vague theology. Led until 1975 by Elijah Muhammad, who focused his message on men whom society had declared irredeemable.

pacifism—Belief that violence is never justified, that peaceful means should always be used to settle disputes.

Selective Service System—United States government agency that administers the draft law. It has draft boards (local claim boards) made up of volunteers who decide claims for conscientious objection, hardship and ministerial deferments. There is also an appeal board system and provision for other exemptions and deferments that are decided by employees of the system.

statute—A law enacted by the legislative branch of a government.

United States Department of Justice—Federal executive department created by Congress in 1870. Headed by the Attorney General of the United States, it enforces federal laws.

World Boxing Association (WBA)—One of the two major controlling bodies of boxing formed in 1962. Its object was to try to break the monopoly of championship titles and contests assumed by the Boxing Department of the New York State Athletic Commission.

Further Reading

About Muhammad Ali:

Bingham, Howard L. *Muhammad Ali: A Thirty-Year Journey.* New York: Simon & Schuster, 1993.

Denenberg, Barry. *The Story of Muhammad Ali: Heavyweight Champion of the World.* Milwaukee, Wis.: Gareth Stevens Inc. 1996.

Diamond, Arthur. *Muhammad Ali.* San Diego, Calif.: Lucent Books, 1995.

Lipsyte, Robert. *Free to Be Muhammad Ali.* New York: Harper & Row, 1978.

Okpaku, Joseph. *Superfight No. II: The Story Behind the Fights Between Muhammad Ali and Joe Frazier.* New Rochelle, N.Y.: Okpaku Communications, 1974.

Riccella, Christopher J. *Muhammad Ali: World Heavyweight Boxing Champion.* Los Angeles: Holloway, 1991.

Schulman, Arlene. *Muhammad Ali: Champion.* Minneapolis, Minn.: Lerner, 1996.

About Boxing:

Andre, Sam. *A Pictorial History of Boxing.* New York: CarolRhoda Publishing Group, 1993.

Ashe, Arthur R. Jr., *A Hard Road to Glory–Boxing: The African-American Athlete in Boxing–Putting the Record Straight: Forgotten Facts.* New York: Amistad Press, 1994.

Brooke-Ball. *Boxing Album: An Illustrated History.* New York: Smithmark Publishing, Inc., 1995.

Jakoubek, Robert. *Jack Johnson.* New York: Chelsea House, 1990.

Suster, Gerald. *Champions of the Ring: The Lives and Times of Boxing's Heavyweight Heroes.* Jersey City, N.J.: Parkwest Publications, 1993.

Vitale, Rugio. *Joe Louis: Boxing Champion.* Los Angeles: Holloway, 1991.

About Conscientious Objection:

Barbour, Hugh and J. William Frost. *The Quakers.* Westport, Conn.: Greenwood Press, 1988.

Icke, Vincent. *Days of Decision: An Oral History of Conscientious Objectors in the Military During Vietnam.* Chicago: LPC InBook, Inc., 1993.

Kohn, Stephen M. *Jailed for Peace: The History of American Draft Law Violators 1658–1985.* Westport, Conn.: Greenwood Press, 1986.

Simons, Donald L. *I Refuse: Memories of a Vietnam War Objector.* Trenton, N.J.: Broken Rifle Press, 1992.

Index